MW01295115

Handy Humanism Handbook

Jen Hancock's

Handy Humanism Handbook

by Jennifer Hancock

Published 2011

Printed by CreateSpace in the United States of
America
Text copyright 2011 by Jennifer Hancock

ISBN-13: 978-1463780654
ISBN-10: 1463780656

http://www.jen-hancock.com

I want to thank my friends and fans for encouraging me to write this book and for their help in editing it.

Special thanks goes out to Ivin Vijoen of Authopublisher.com, without whom I would never have thought to write this book.

And of course, super special thanks goes out to my hubby for the incredible love and support he has gives to me every day and for the encouragement he gives me to stick at it when I am thinking I perhaps should be doing something else.

Table of Contents:

Introduction

This book is written to provide a quick overview of the philosophy of Humanism for the average Joe or Jane. I don't care which actually because I'm a Humanist and I don't judge people based on their gender or skin color or any other arbitrary characteristic. So, let's revise that introductory statement. This book is for the average human, regardless of his or her name, who wants to learn more about Humanism.

Humanism is one of the most influential and yet most maligned philosophies of all time. Unfortunately, most people don't know anything about it. To make matters worse, there are a lot of people who are already Humanists and just don't know it yet because no one has ever taken the time to properly introduce them to the philosophy.

I intend to change that with this book. Consider yourself introduced.

No Proselytizing

I am not out to proselytize for Humanism. This is a philosophy. Some of you may agree with what is written here and some of you may not. If you do, I hope this book will help clarify your personal philosophy and that it will help you to be more confident about positively declaring yourself as a Humanist.

If, however, you read this book and it annoys you and you find you don't agree with anything in it, that's fine. Not everyone is a Humanist. I'm not out to change your mind. There is no dogma to Humanism. This philosophy either makes sense to you or it doesn't. If it turns out this doesn't make sense to you, what I hope you take away from this book is a basic level of knowledge about the Humanist philosophy so that you can better understand what motivates us Humanists.

Finally, there are those who will agree with only some of this book. Again, that's fine too. Humanism is a philosophy. You are free to take from it what you want and leave the rest. Usually when this happens people agree with our morality but disagree with our rejection of the supernatural. If this describes you, you can consider yourself humanistically inclined if that makes you happy.

What You Need To Know

This book is designed to be a short and hopefully sweet introduction to the philosophy of Humanism, hitting on all the important bits including:
- what Humanism is
- what we Humanists care about
- how we go about solving our problems
- why we believe our way of thinking about the world is better than the alternatives. and

- why, if you are a Humanist, you should probably admit it to yourself and to others

Because Humanism arises in every culture and in every time, there is, quite literally, more information than you could ever possibly read to help you explore the philosophy further. There are also national and local organizations of Humanists that you can reach out to and get to know. In addition, there are many online groups you can participate in. Whatever floats your boat and works for you. You can also choose to do nothing with the information you read in this book.

Just as an FYI, if you do want to explore the philosophy in more detail, I suggest you buy my other book, *The Humanist Approach to Happiness: Practical Wisdom.* It goes into more detail about the practical aspects of what it is like to live life as a Humanist. It's an easy read and people like it, so check it out.

I also created an Introduction to Humanism video series, which is available on YouTube or as a DVD. Visit www.jen-hancock.com for more information on either of these resources.

But enough of the self-promotion. Let's talk about Humanism.

What Is Humanism And Why Should I Care?

To put it simply, Humanism is one of the most powerful forces for positive social change on the planet. Some of the most famous and influential people in our society have been and continue to be Humanists. The Humanist philosophy provided the foundation for most of the social and civil justice movements of the past century as well as providing the philosophical foundation for democracy and science.

Quite literally, if it weren't for Humanists, Europe would still be in the Dark Ages. America would probably have not been "discovered" by Europeans and everyone everywhere would still be trying to cook with fire. And no, I'm not exaggerating.

The modern world has been shaped and made possible by the dominance of Humanist ideas. Which is exactly why it's so stunning that most people have no idea what it is.

So What Is Humanism?

One of the main reasons Humanism is so poorly understood is that it has no standard definition. Yet, it is instantly recognizable once you grasp its central ideas. It is a very simple philosophy that has some very profound implications for how you view your place in the universe. As one of my friends in Saudi Arabia once pointed out, it isn't rocket science. If you spend just a little bit of time thinking about what morality and ethics mean to us as humans without the prescriptions of religion and divine revelation, Humanism is probably what you are going to come up with.

Regardless, this is a book about Humanism so perhaps I should provide you with something more concrete to wrap your mind around.

Defining Humanism

The American Humanist Association defines Humanism as "a progressive philosophy of life, that without supernaturalism, affirms our ability and responsibility to lead ethical lives of personal fulfillment that aspire to the greater good of Humanity." (http://www.americanhumanist.org)

In other words, it's a way of thinking about ethics that emphasizes both our personal development and our moral obligations. As I like to say: live life, love other people and leave the world a better place.

Or To Put It Another Way

According to the International Humanist and Ethical Union's Amsterdam Declaration of 2002,

"Humanism is the outcome of a long tradition of free thought that has inspired many of the world's great thinkers and creative artists and gave rise to science itself." According the IHEU (http://www.iheu.org) there are seven fundamental elements of Humanism:

- **Humanism is ethical.** Humanists have a duty to care for all of humanity including future generations.
- **Humanism is rational.** Humanism advocates the application of the methods of science and free inquiry to the problems of human welfare.
- **Humanism supports democracy and human rights.** The principles of democracy and human rights can be applied to many human relationships and are not restricted to methods of government.
- **Humanism insists that personal liberty must be combined with social responsibility.** Humanism ventures to build a world on the idea of the free person responsible to society.
- **Humanism is a response to the widespread demand for an alternative to dogmatic religion.** Humanism recognizes that reliable knowledge of the world and ourselves arises through a continuing process of observation, evaluation and revision.
- **Humanism values artistic creativity and imagination.** Humanism affirms the importance of literature, music, and the visual

and performing arts for personal development and fulfillment.
- **Humanism is a life stance aimed at maximizing our personal fulfillment through the cultivation of ethical and creative living.** It offers an ethical and rational means of addressing the challenges of our time.

Keep It Simple Stupid

By now your head is probably spinning. One of the problems we Humanists have in explaining our philosophy is that it is deceptively simple, yet wonderfully complex. There is no easy way to describe it.

Regardless, I will give you a synopsis in plain English, understanding that we will be going into more detail on these basic elements in the following chapters.

Humanism is a philosophy that is primarily focused on how we as individuals can be good human beings. We seek to be ethical, moral and compassionate people in all that we do. However, we also understand that good moral reasoning requires us to think clearly and rationally about the problems we face. So Humanists are as much concerned with how we think, as we are concerned with what we think about. To that end we practice the related skills of freethought, critical thinking and logic.

Humanists are firmly convinced that we are in control of our own destinies and that we can choose to act in a way that will improve our lives and the lives of others. In other words, we refuse to be victims of fate. For this reason, Humanism is a philosophy that focuses on the future. We are not content with the status quo as we are always pushing ourselves to make things better.

How we define "better" is critical to understanding the philosophy of Humanism. Humanists judge outcomes using a compassion-based morality and we are totally unapologetic about that. If it helps humans, it is a good outcome. If it hurts, it is bad. Absent from our thinking and reasoning is anything that could be considered supernatural or religious.

We do not consider religious or supernatural ideas to be a sound basis for moral reasoning. Our concern for the welfare of others is sufficient and we have no need for any external or supernatural sanction for our moral values. We are, in fact, convinced that religious reasoning, however well intentioned it may be, tends to cause more harm than good because it encourages dogmatic adherence to a set of rules instead of acknowledging the necessity of judging each situation on its own merits.

In other words, without supernaturalism, Humanists seek to lead ethical lives of personal fulfillment that aspire to the greater good of humanity. And we do this by applying reason and logic to our feelings of compassion with a determination to actively work to make things better not just for ourselves, but for everyone.

A Short History Of Humanism

The next question is: how long has Humanism been around? The answer is that Humanism has probably been around as long as there have been humans. And as long as it has been around, there have been people who demonize it. Which is interesting because, really, it's not like Humanism is some radical idea. Well, actually, it is. More on that later.

My point is that people keep re-inventing Humanism for themselves. All it takes is for a compassionate person to spend some time thinking about morality, the universe, and everything without religion and he or she will usually come up with something that is either Humanism or closely related to it. And this process is happening all the time and has probably been happening throughout human history.

The problem is that we don't really have historical records going back to the dawn of humanity. What we know about Humanist philosophies is limited to the historical era, otherwise known as the last 7,000 to 10,000 years.

Here's what we know. In every culture that is studied, including those that rely on an oral tradition (as opposed to written), we see evidence of Humanist thought. We see it in the writings of the ancient Sumerians and of the ancient Egyptians and in the oral traditions of American Indians and Arctic nomads.

However, when we get to about 600 BCE (Before the Common Era), we start to see specifically Humanist writings begin to appear all over the world. This development is probably more a function of us actually having these writings to refer to rather than the lack of such thinkers earlier.

For a really great resource, check out www.humanistictexts.org which provides a wonderful collection of Humanistic writings from various time periods and from all parts of the globe.

Let's review some of the main forms of Humanism that have developed over time.

Ancient Humanism

In India:

There are two major philosophies that came out of ancient India that are either Humanist or Humanistic in nature. Carvaka and Buddhism.

Let's start with Carvaka. This philosophy arose in India around 600 BCE and is both a skeptical and rationalistic philosophy. It rejected the supernatural and the Vedas and emphasized that this was the only life we have, so make the best of it.

> *While life is yours live joyously;*
> *No one can avoid Death's searching eye:*
> *When this body of ours is burnt,*

How can it ever return again?

Buddhism is often considered a Humanistic philosophy and many modern Humanists practice Buddhist meditation as a way to train and calm their minds. The aspects of Buddhism that are most like Humanism are its emphasis on finding balance and on compassion.

> *Happiness comes when your work and words are of benefit to yourself and others.*

> *There are only two mistakes one can make along the road to truth: not going all the way, and not starting.*

In China:

In ancient China, there were at least two great Humanist teachers whose knowledge survives to this day. As in India, one is more famous than the other. These two philosophic teachers were Confucius and Mo Tzu.

Confucius lived around 500 BCE and was a civil servant turned philosopher/teacher. His philosophy was as much concerned with cultivating virtue in individuals as it was with creating a virtuous government.

From The Great Learning:

Acting according to our humanity provides the true path through life. Wisdom from the past helps us learn how to follow this path.

From the Analects:

Tsze-lu asked what constituted the superior man. Confucius answered,

"The cultivation of himself in reverential carefulness."
"And is this all?"
"He cultivates himself so as to give rest to others."
"And is this all?"
"He cultivates himself so as to give rest to all the people."

Mo Tzu was also a civil servant turned philosopher/teacher. He lived around 400 BCE and taught universal love and meritocracy rather than aristocracy.

Mo Tzu said: The purpose of the Humanist is to be found in procuring benefits for the world and eliminating its calamities.

Now, how is a doctrine to be examined? Mo Tzu said: Some standard of judgment must be established. To expound a doctrine without regard to the standard is similar to determining the directions of sunrise and sunset on a revolving potter's wheel. By such a means, the distinction of right and wrong,

*benefit and harm, cannot be known. Therefore
there must be three tests.
What are the three tests?
Mo Tzu said: Its basis, its verifiability, and its
applicability.*

The Greeks:

The ancient Greeks had a lot of Humanists and
humanistically inclined philosophers. For the sake of
brevity, I am going to focus on just three. Socrates,
Democritus and Epicurus.

The most famous of these three is Socrates. As he is
considered to be the founder of Western philosophy,
we will start with him. He lived around 400 BCE and
is most famous for his ethics and methods of
discourse.

> *Some one will say: And are you not ashamed,
> Socrates, of a course of life which is likely to
> bring you to an untimely end? To him I may
> fairly answer: There you are mistaken: a man
> who is good for anything ought not to
> calculate the chance of living or dying; he
> ought only to consider whether in doing
> anything he is doing right or wrong—acting
> the part of a good man or of a bad.*

Democritus is pre-Socratic, meaning he lived before
Socrates. He is considered to be the father of modern

science because of his work on atoms. He was also an ardent defender of democracy as a form of government. Regardless, some of the most Humanistic quotes from ancient Greece come from Democritus so I'm including several here just because I love what he had to say so much.

> *Men find happiness neither by means of the body nor through possessions, but through uprightness and wisdom.*

> *It is hard to fight desire; but to control it is the sign of a reasonable man. Violent desire for one thing blinds the soul to all others. Immoderate desire is the mark of a child, not a man. If your desires are not great, a little will seem much to you; for small appetite makes poverty equivalent to wealth.*

> *Virtue does not consist of avoiding wrongdoing, but in having no wish to do wrong. It is a great thing, when one is in adversity, to think of duty. Refrain from crimes not through fear but through duty.*

> *Believe not everything, but only what is proven: the former is foolish, the latter the act of a sensible man. Fools are shaped by the gifts of chance, but those who understand these things, by the gifts of wisdom.*

Epicurus lived around 300 BCE and believed man's purpose was to live a happy and peaceful life. He believed that good and evil are best judged by whether they bring pleasure or pain. His name is, to this day, synonymous with the pursuit of pleasure in the Western world.

> *Death does not concern us, because as long as we exist, death is not here. And when it does come, we no longer exist.*

> *It is folly for a man to pray to the gods for that which he has the power to obtain by himself.*

Fast Forward

Rather than continue on with a litany of Humanist thinkers and writers, I'm going to give you my fast forward version of Humanist history. What follows is a quick overview of the high points as I see them.

The Golden Age Of Islam

Let's fast forward to medieval Europe. It's in the Dark Ages. Christianity is dominant. It's basically a land lit only by fire. But in Arabia, Africa and Asia, they are experiencing a golden age. This period, known as the Golden Age of Islam, lasted from about 700 CE (Common Era - used to be referred to as AD) to the 16th century. This was a period when scholars were studying all the ancient traditions from China, Persia, Greece and India. And yes, they included the various Humanist traditions as part of their study.

Because of the relative freedom of the sciences, Islamic culture flourished during this time.

Many people are surprised to find that there are indeed Humanist traditions within the greater community of Islam. The fact is that there were full-on secular Humanists of great renown living during this period. For instance, Abu Bakr Al-Razi, a famous medical writer of the 9th century, believed that reason alone could give us certain knowledge, that all claims of revelation were false, and that religions were dangerous.

Anyway, what is important to our understanding of the history of Humanism is that the scholars of Islam during its Golden Age were excited by, and were willing to learn from, other cultures.

> *"We should not be ashamed to acknowledge truth from whatever source it comes to us, even if it is brought to us by former generations and foreign peoples. For him who seeks the truth there is nothing of higher value than truth itself."*
> *- Al-Kindi (c. 801-66)*

Islamic scholars spent a lot of time copying, translating and studying the works of the "ancients." And because they did that, those texts were available for Europeans to "rediscover" when they finally decided that they'd had enough of living in ignorance. Which brings us to the European Renaissance.

The Renaissance

If you didn't learn about the European Renaissance in school or can't remember much about it except that it was in Europe and marked the end of the Dark Ages, here is what you need to know.

The Renaissance was a cultural movement that spanned a few hundred years. The hallmark of this period in Europe was that people started to take an interest in learning things again. Specifically, they were interested in learning the "classics," which to them meant the ancient Greeks. The problem is that once people start learning they tend to become voracious learners. As a result, over the course of a few centuries, Europe went from being a backwater place to being the center of learning and culture in the world. This didn't make the Muslims too happy, but that's another story.

Anyway, it was during the Renaissance when the term Humanist started to be used. A Renaissance Humanist was basically a scholar of the humanities. In hindsight, it was inevitable that the Renaissance Humanists, as they started to learn more and more about what other people thought and about the history of Christianity itself, would start to question the official dogma of the Catholic Church. As you might expect, the Catholic Church hierarchy wasn't exactly happy about this development. Which brings us to the Reformation.

The Reformation

As learning became more widespread, the problem of controlling what people thought about religion got bigger and bigger. This struggle eventually resulted in the Reformation.

There were a wide variety of reasons why European reformers wanted to reform the Catholic Church. Some reasons were political; some were intellectual; some were theological. There was also the fact that the Catholic Church was seriously corrupt. Regardless, people started to break away from the authority of the Catholic Church and Humanism was often invoked as a way to declare intellectual independence from the Church. There were wars, people died, and at the end of the day, people were basically free to believe whatever they wanted, more or less.

Enlightenment

Once people in Europe had freed their minds from Catholic control, scientists were able to actually pursue truth where it led and not just where the Catholic Church thought it should go. I like to think of the Enlightenment as a period when, having won the basic right of freedom of belief, intellectuals were now free to focus their attention on expanding scientific knowledge and on pursuing social issues that concerned them.

The Enlightenment was a mid-18th century

movement and the hallmark of it was the idea that human reason was the only way to discern truth. So critical thinking, the challenging of arbitrary authority and a strong belief in the power of rationality were hallmarks of the period. According to Immanuel Kant, the Enlightenment represented *"Mankind's final coming of age, the emancipation of the human consciousness from an immature state of ignorance and error."*

This period, which was basically a Humanist revolution, culminated in the American Revolution. As I wrote earlier, Humanist ideas are pretty simple and straightforward, but that is precisely what makes them so revolutionary and radical.

Modern Age

Many historians think the modern age of Humanism began with the publication of Thomas Paine's *Age of Reason* in the years 1794 to 1807 (when the final draft was done). This book was a product of the Enlightenment. It openly rejected the supernaturalism of the Bible. But more importantly, it directly attacked the authority of the Bible itself, treating the book as one would any other piece of literature. It was pretty scandalous, but it was also a best seller.

After that, more and more people started to write about the need for a morality based on something other than supernatural beliefs and by 1853 the British Humanistic Religious Society was founded.

In 1877 the word Humanist was used to describe Felix Adler, the founder of the Ethical Culture Society, which was formed to promote what is now known as Ethical Humanism.

In the 1920s, some Unitarian ministers started preaching a pragmatic nonreligious philosophy they called "Humanism," and in 1929 Rev. Charles Francis Potter founded the First Humanist Society of New York. His advisory board consisted of Albert Einstein, Julian Huxley, Helen Keller and John Dewey.

In 1933 the first Humanist Manifesto was written and signed and in 1941 the American Humanist Association was founded. In 1952 the International Humanist and Ethical Union was founded. And that pretty much brings us up to the present, historically speaking.

So What Has Humanism Done For You Lately?

Well, if you like freedom of belief, then you can thank Humanists like Erasmus, whose work during the Renaissance laid the philosophic foundation for the Reformation. If you like democracy, you can thank Humanists such as John Locke, a key figure of the Enlightenment. If you like equal rights for all, then you can thank Humanists like A. Phillip Randolph and Helen Keller, who were instrumental in securing equal rights for minorities, women and the disabled.

If you like having vaccines, antibiotics and modern medicine, you should absolutely thank a Humanist. The list of Humanists who have made significant contributions to science and medicine is rather long and includes Crick and Watson (DNA) and Jonas Salk (polio vaccine). In fact, 22 currently living Nobel Laureates in science consider themselves to be Humanists.

As I said at the beginning of this book, modern life, as we know it, would not have been possible without Humanists. Basically, if it weren't for Humanists, we would probably all still be living in the Dark Ages.

Well, actually, that's assuming your ancestors were living in Europe, because it turns out that the rest of the world wasn't experiencing a dark age during the period we in the West call the Dark Ages. However, if there weren't any Humanists anywhere, Islam probably wouldn't have had its Golden Age at all. If it had not been for Humanists exerting their influence somewhere, it's pretty safe to assume that everywhere would have been in a dark age except we wouldn't know about it because, well, we wouldn't know any different.

Regardless, the point is that if we are considering the impact Humanism has had on the history of Western culture and by extension the rest of the world, the European Renaissance, fueled by the philosophy of Humanism, had a tremendous impact on the world. We might not agree on whether that impact was positive or negative given all the expansion, exploration and exploitation that went on, but it certainly caused dramatic changes to occur just about everywhere. The quality of the science from the period of the Enlightenment, again, driven by Humanists in Europe and their counterparts around the world, gave us things like electricity and modern medicine. It is because of Humanists that we aren't all still trying to toast our bread over an open fire. Point made.

Gratuitous Name Dropping

A lot of really famous and influential people are Humanists. In fact, if you remember a philosopher from ancient history, that is probably because he was a Humanist. The great thinkers and doers throughout history are often considered "great" precisely because of their Humanism. We didn't just have Socrates, Buddha and Confucius. We also had Marcus Aurelius (Roman Emperor and Stoic), Thomas Jefferson (President and Deist) and Voltaire (philosophical satirist and human rights activist).

However, there is one eensy weensy teeny little problem. Prior to the mid-1800s, no one called themselves a Humanist even if they were and the philosophy wasn't even described as a philosophy until the early 1900s. So while we know from their writings that these "greats" were Humanists or humanistically inclined, they didn't actually call themselves Humanists or label their philosophy Humanism. As it is intellectually dishonest to ascribe a philosophy to people without their expressed consent, we can't actually claim authoritatively that any of them were Humanists. The best we can do is say they appear to be Humanists or that they were promoting a Humanistic philosophy in hindsight.

However, since the advent of modern Humanism, there has been a growing number of people who do and did in fact label themselves as Humanists. The list of notables within the Humanist community is quite long and quite impressive. I am providing you with a short list of famous modern Humanists to give you an idea of who all we are. Please realize that this list is in no way exhaustive. I just picked a few in each category so you would understand the extent to which we Humanists play an influential role in our societies and cultures. If you don't know someone on this list, please look them up.

Scientists:

Albert Einstein, physicist, was a founding member of the First Humanist Society of New York and a member of the American Humanist Association.

Carl Sagan, astronomer, was a member of the American Humanist Association and received their Humanist of the Year award in 1981. He was also named Humanist Laureate for the International Academy of Humanism.

B.F. Skinner, psychologist, was Humanist of the Year in 1972 and was a signer of Humanist Manifesto II.

Francis Crick and James Watson, biochemists, were both named Humanist Laureates by the International Academy of Humanism.

Linus Pauling, chemist, was Humanist of the Year in 1961.

Jonas Salk, medical researcher, won that honor in 1976.

Writers:

Isaac Asimov served as honorary president of the American Humanist Association from 1985 until his death in 1992. He was named Humanist of the Year in 1984.

Arthur C. Clarke, was a distinguished supporter of the British Humanist Association and was named a Humanist Laureate by the International Academy of Humanism.

Kurt Vonnegut was the honorary president of the American Humanist Association from 1992 until his death in 2007. He was a signer of Humanist Manifesto III, *Humanism and it's Aspirations* and was named Humanist of the Year in 1992.

Gore Vidal is the current honorary president of the American Humanist Association.

Joyce Carol Oates was named Humanist of the Year in 2007 by the American Humanist Association.

Christopher Hitchens is a well known and much loved Humanist and is a Humanist Laureate of the International Academy of Humanism.

Julian Huxley was not only the founder of the first Humanist Society of New York, he also helped found and presided over the creation of the International Humanist and Ethical Union.

Entertainers

Gene Roddenberry was a member of the American Humanist Association and is considered one of the most influential yet unheralded Humanists of the 20th century.

Rod Serling was a member of the Unitarian Universalists and considered himself to be a naturalistic Humanist.

Comedian Steve Allen was named Humanist Laureate by the International Academy of Humanism and was the honorary chairman of the Council for Secular Humanism until his death.

Joss Whedon, the creator of Buffy the Vampire Slayer and Firefly, is a Humanist. In early 2009 he gave a presentation to the Humanist Chaplaincy at Harvard about the importance of Humanism.

Björn Ulvaeus of ABBA is a member of the Swedish Humanist Association.

Peter Ustinov was named Humanist Laureate of the International Academy of Humanism.

Social Activists:

Helen Caldicott a famous anti-nuclear advocate was the American Humanist Association's Humanist of the Year in 1982.

A. Phillip Randolph, the civil rights activist, received the American Humanist Association's Humanist of the Year award in 1970 and was a signatory to Humanist Manifesto I.

Helen Keller was a member of the American Humanist Association and was a founding member of the First Humanist Society of New York, along with Albert Einstein.

Margaret Sanger was the Humanist of the Year for the American Humanist Association in 1957.

Faye Wattleton received the Humanist of the Year award in 1986.

Andrei Sakharov received the Humanist of the Year award in 1980.

No, I'm Not A Satanist.

Thanks For Asking

In this chapter, I am going to answer some of the most common questions we Humanists get. I decided to write this chapter because there is a lot of misinformation out there and the sort of outright lies that are told about Humanism would make you think that Humanists are evil and are actively working for Satan. It isn't unusual for Humanists to be blamed for pretty much everything that's wrong with the world. And while I know that we aren't the only group blamed for things that have absolutely nothing to do with us, it does get old very quickly.

Anyway, if you are bold enough to tell a complete stranger that you are a Humanist, you are likely to get one of two basic reactions. The first and most common response is that you get a blank look followed by a bit of curiosity and several questions.

The second response is less common but a bit more funny or depressing depending on your mood at the time, and that reaction appears to be a mix of "fear of the Devil" mingled with a general sense of: "Gee, this person seems nice."

Stupid Questions

Which brings us to the stupid questions people who think we might be Satanists ask. It turns out there are a lot of really stupid questions. The person who first claimed there were no stupid questions obviously never had to endure the questions we Humanists get all the time. After all, our philosophy is without supernaturalism, which means it is also without a god. And all good Christians "know" that if you are without their god, you must be with Satan.

This leads to some well meaning, but rather silly questions. It isn't the fault of the person asking the question. Most haven't met a Humanist before. Given the level of misinformation being spread about Humanism by religious leaders all across the world, it isn't too surprising that when a person of faith finds out that we aren't the demons they were told we would be, they are surprised. It's natural in such circumstances to have a lot of questions.

There is no better way to dispel the myths about Humanism than to actually just answer these misinformed questions. So...let's get started.

Are We Satanists?

No. We are without supernaturalism. If Satan is considered to be a supernatural being, then he is irrelevant to us. We'd have to believe such a being existed in order to worship it. We don't, so we don't.

But that isn't saying much. Even Satanists don't believe in the literal existence of Satan. Even though Satanism is a secular belief system just as Humanism is, many of their principal beliefs are incompatible with Humanism. For instance, Satanists hold an extremely negative view of Humanity and advocate for vengeance rather than compassion. So no, we aren't Satanists.

Aren't You Afraid Of Going To Hell?

No we are not. Again, we are without supernaturalism. Those of us who are Atheists don't believe such a place exists. For the record, it's really hard to work up fear for something you don't believe exists. Additionally, Humanists strive to be moral people. The idea that we would be punished in spite of being good just because of our lack of belief seems incredibly unjust to us. Most Humanists would refuse to worship a being that unjust. Regardless, the reason we aren't afraid of going to Hell is because we don't believe Hell exists outside of Michigan. (FYI, there is a town called Hell in Michigan. I wasn't ragging on the good folks from the Great Lakes State.)

But You Have To Believe In Something!

No you do not. You don't have to do anything you don't want to. Yes, there are consequences to what you believe, but the choice is yours to believe or not.

Don't You Just Replace God With Man?

No. Humanists are first and foremost realists and we realize that Humans aren't all that wonderful. We don't worship humans instead of a god because we don't worship anything at all. What we are saying and advocating is that good and bad are best judged through the lens of human compassion. If it helps, it is good. If it hurts, it is bad. Either the gods, if they exist, agree with this moral formulation or they don't. Ultimately though, we don't feel we need their approval for our morality.

Brilliant Questions

Not all the questions we get are stupid. Some are actually quite brilliant. These are the questions that deal with morality and our place in the universe. We Humanists love to answer these sorts of questions because they mean the person asking them is starting to grasp what the philosophy is all about and are just trying to figure out what it encompasses and whether they agree with it or not.

Where Does Morality Come From If Not From God?

This is a very important question to ask. And the answer is quite simple. We evolved to be moral creatures. Most humans everywhere in the world value the same things: honesty, compassion, and responsibility. We almost all have a sense of justice and our sense of justice is almost always based on our feelings of compassion for others. I know some religious people say that compassion is the spark of the divine within us. We Humanists think that we evolved to have emotions and that these emotions are sufficient for us to determine what is good and what is bad. Ultimately, I don't care where these emotions come from, just that you fully develop and nurture your compassion for others. The Humanist perspective is that it is our compassion, whether god-given or evolved, that helps us determine right from wrong.

Do You Think Humans Are Superior To All The Other Animals?

No. We hold a scientific viewpoint, which is that a human is an animal that has evolved some pretty nifty tricks. The common mistake made when contemplating the consequences of evolution is to view evolution as a progression: to assume that some organisms are higher up the evolutionary ladder than others and that they are somehow better than the others as a result. What evolution actually teaches us is that organisms are like leaves on a tree. All the leaves are unique, yet they all grew out of the same original seed that grew into the tree. How could you possibly say that one leaf is superior to the other leaves on this tree? You can't.

Organisms, within an evolutionary framework, can only be judged as successful or unsuccessful given how well they exploit the niche they live in and how long they are able to survive as a species unchanged. In this framework there are some worms that have been around unchanged for billions of years. They are incredibly successful, way more so than humans who have only been around a short time, evolutionarily speaking.

But that doesn't mean we Humanists don't think humans are super cool. We do. We are actually rather fond of our own species. But, long story short:no, we don't view humans as superior to the other species we share planet Earth with. We don't think we have dominion over them. That's a Biblical concept, not a Humanist one.

Why Do We Need Another Ism?

While most isms divide humans, Humanism unites us. It makes us feel connected to all the other humans on the planet. We aren't alone. We have an entire family of humans, around 7 billion actually. That's pretty amazing. And all of them are real people, with real lives, real families, real struggles and real loves. Just like you. What's even more amazing is that in addition to our fellow humans, we are also connected to all the life on the planet. We can't survive without them.

While most isms divide and narrow your thinking, Humanism, because it's based on the reality of who and what humans are, is actually mind expanding and connecting. It is the only ism that has the ability to transcend all the other isms and bring us together into one human family.

So no. We don't need another ism. We just need Humanism, in my humble opinion, anyway.

Religion Doesn't Hold A Monopoly On Morality

One of the biggest lies told about Humanism is that it is amoral, in other words, that it is without morals. The argument that is made is that morality comes from god(s) so if you are without a god you must be without morals. This is a particularly nasty lie because, as it turns out, Humanism is first and foremost an ethical system. One of the first organizations to promote Humanism in America was the Ethical Culture Society. It has the word ethical in its name. Seriously, we care a lot about morality and ethics.

Morality isn't necessarily tied to religion, and religious groups don't hold a monopoly on teaching about morality and ethics. As my father always says, no group corners the market on stupidity. There are stupid and immoral people in every group. The fact that there are priests who have raped children and atheists who have lent a helping hand to their neighbors in distress is proof of this concept.

It isn't religious belief that makes you moral. It is your personal adherence to a moral system that makes you moral. You can talk a good talk all you want, but at the end of the day, your morality is going to be judged on how you actually act.

Our goal, as Humanists, is to be good people who do good things for our fellow humans. We don't do this because of fear of punishment after we die. We do it because being a good person has benefits here and now, and because being a good person aids in our feelings of personal happiness, and we would rather be happy than sad.

To explore this concept in more detail I suggest you get my other book: The Humanist Approach to Happiness: Practical Wisdom. (http://happiness.jen-hancock.com)

In the meantime, let's move on.

Humanist Ethics Are Human Ethics

So what are Humanist ethics? Well, I'm glad you asked. Humanist ethics are human ethics. They are not only derived from our natural needs, wants and desires, they are also fairly universal. It doesn't matter where you go or what you believe or don't believe about gods, the universe and everything, most humans value the same things and our ethics, as humans, are fairly standard across the globe.

If you are religious, you might ascribe this similarity of concerns to your god's divine spark within us. For the non-religious, it is sufficient to say that we evolved to have the emotions that cause us to judge some things as inherently right and some things as inherently wrong. What matters is that the primary emotion that leads us to make these value judgments appears to be compassion.

We Really Care

Humanism is a value system that bases its morality on our feelings of human compassion. We don't apologize for that. We feel that there is no better way of making moral judgments about what is right and what is wrong than compassion. While ours isn't the only system to base our morals on compassion, we appear to be the only one that does so without the need of any other external justification. In other words, we don't need a god to tell us a compassion-based morality is good. We already know that ourselves.

Humanist morality isn't just about saying, "Well, my compassion tells me that helping people is good and hurting people is wrong." We can also judge whether this system works by looking at the outcomes created by this system. Things are judged as being good or bad based on how we are affected, how our communities are affected, and the how the world in which we live is affected.

Humanist thinkers throughout history have found that a compassion-based morality not only benefits us as individuals as we practice compassion, but that our communities are improved. It simply leads to better outcomes, and that's all the justification we need to adopt and adhere to such a value system.

The Down Side

This isn't to say that a compassion-based ethics is perfect or easy. It isn't. Even if you choose to use compassion as your moral compass, it is very hard to sort out what is moral or immoral when the needs of one person must be weighed against the needs of another.

Different people utilizing compassion as the basis for their decision-making will often come to drastically different decisions about what is moral and what isn't. The abortion debate is a prime example of this. Pretty much everyone is basing his or her opinion on compassion. Whether we primarily feel compassion for the unborn child or for the mother or for both determines how we feel about this issue.

Situational Ethics

Humanists consider our morality to be situational. We recognize that it doesn't matter how good any given rule is, there will always be instances when that rule should be broken in order to do the right and moral thing. Situational ethics are contrasted with absolute ethics, which hold that there are no situations that ever arise where our values are in conflict with one another so there is never a situation where it might be considered ethical to abandon one of our values in favor of another.

The typical hypothetical example given when discussing the concept of situational ethics is when you are asked to consider whether it is okay to kill one person in order to save the lives of thousands or millions of people. Almost every human on the planet responds to this hypothetical by saying that it is moral to kill one to save thousands, but that we'd rather not be put in a situation to have to make that decision. Because of this, Humanists acknowledge that all human ethics are situational, whether they are recognized as situational or not.

Adherents to absolute ethical systems scoff at this example saying such situations never actually arise in real life. Yet, they do. The killing of Osama Bin Laden by the United States is a perfect real-life example of the "kill one to save others" moral dilemma. Whether you agree with the killing of Bin Laden or not, this real-life moral dilemma required us all to consider which of our values to invoke in this particular situation. In other words, situations do arise where our ethical system is inadequate and we have to use our own judgment, and very few of us enjoyed thinking through this dilemma at all. The point is that if our values were absolute we wouldn't have had to struggle with this dilemma at all. Situational ethics are the human norm whether we like it or not.

It Takes Some Effort

While I didn't want to pass judgment on the Bin Laden affair I do want to point out that no matter how good your moral values are you need to be prepared to make ethical and moral decisions when what is right and what is wrong isn't clear. In other words, you need a moral framework for dealing with the exceptions to your normal rules of morality. Humanists solve these exceptions by trying to figure out what will do the most good and the least harm. And yes, this does require you to think and do your research.

No one said moral reasoning was easy. To be a truly moral person, you have to be willing to put some effort into it. And this is why Humanists consider education and critical thinking skills to be so important to moral development.

On Being Good

As for being a good person: it isn't enough to want to do good. You can only be a good person by doing good things. What is the value are your professed morals if you don't put them into action? A failure to act according to your moral values is a failure in your morality.

This might seem like we are highly judgmental people, but actually our focus on morality is a personal practice. This isn't about preaching to others how they should behave. It's about reminding ourselves how we ought to behave. It's what we aspire to as individuals.

Humanist morality is first and foremost a personal choice. It is what we expect from ourselves that defines us as Humanists. We know that when we adhere to our morals, we feel better and are able to achieve good things, not only for ourselves but for others as well. When we fail to live up to our own high moral standards, we understand that we are diminished as a result.

We Humanists expect a lot from ourselves when it comes to our own personal behavior. If we mess up, which everyone does occasionally, we know that unless we take responsibility for our actions and actively work to fix things, our guilt will gnaw away at us. It isn't enough for us to say we are sorry. We actually have to make an effort to not make that same mistake again.

Judge Not Lest You Be Judged

Granted, while our morality is mostly focused on how we as Humanists choose to behave, that doesn't mean we aren't going to judge the behavior of others. We have to. In our lives we all come across people who aren't nice, and who aren't ethical. If we choose not to judge others, we will be unable to keep ourselves safe from unscrupulous individuals and that will make it harder for us to navigate successfully through life. We have to have some way of judging whether people are treating us ethically or not.

Which leads to the reason why I think Humanism is so great. We judge people based on how they actually act!

It's amazing this is still considered a radical idea. We aren't concerned with how people look, what their skin color is, how they did their hair, how rich they are, or even what they profess to believe. We care about how they act. We've found that judging people as individuals based on how they act and not on some other arbitrary accident of birth or social grouping gives us a really good indication of how they will act in the future!

By judging people on how they actually act, we are better able to navigate the maze of life. All I'm saying is that you might want to rethink some of your biases and bigotries and give it a try and see how it turns out for you.

Long story short, when it comes to morality, Humanism isn't concerned with talking a good talk. You actually have to walk the good walk to be considered an ethical person. If you fail, we won't tell you that you are going to Hell. We will simply choose to avoid you in the future.

Your actions have consequences; so choose your actions wisely. If you choose not to be an ethical person, that's your business and you are the one who will have to deal with the consequences of that choice. Just know that the rest of us will be doing our best to steer clear of you.

Religion Isn't Helping

Which brings me to the last topic related to morality. Believe it or not, our lack of reliance on religion and supernatural beliefs is actually a huge part of the reason why we feel it is so important to be a moral person in the first place. If this is the only life we get and it turns out that there are no gods, then how we behave towards each other here and now matters greatly. In fact, it is everything. To put it bluntly, while we recognize there are some wonderful people of faith, we feel that faith, in general, is more a hindrance than a help when it comes to encouraging people to behave morally.

Religion's emphasis on an afterlife takes our focus away from the here and now. Instead of thinking about how we can help each other, the focus becomes how to do the will of the gods. Instead of thinking about the immediate consequences of our actions, we are told to only think about the consequences in a potential afterlife that, let's face it, no one, not even the most devout believer, is actually certain exists.

Instead of seeking forgiveness from our fellow humans, we are told we only need to seek the forgiveness from a god we have never met, never seen, and of whom we have no direct knowledge.

Religion may encourage us to be moral but its tendency towards dogmatism actually hinders moral development. There are many studies that back that up. See Israel Wahlman's study on dogmatism and moral development for an example. Put simply and bluntly, there are better ways to teach morality than religion.

It's A Radical Idea

The other problem with religion is that certain forms or beliefs do not promote compassion-based ethics at all. While most people consider compassion-based ethics to be, well, basic, even going so far as to ascribe this sort of ethics to their religion, some devout believers do not. It doesn't matter what the religion is, devout individuals who prefer an absolute ethic based on their god's will often reject compassion outright. In this framework compassion is considered irrelevant because it's pretty clear that whatever their god is, its will involves a certain amount of suffering and so we cannot judge something as good based on compassion. If suffering occurs, it must be good because a god must have ordained it.

While this disagreement on what the proper basis for morality is doesn't bother Humanists much, it matters tremendously to people who hold an absolutist non-compassion-based ethic. Believe it or not, conservative religious leaders see our unapologetic adherence to a compassion-based situational ethic as the most radical aspect of our philosophy. It threatens the very foundation of their beliefs. And it is on this basis that they demonize Humanism, trying to claim that because it isn't based on their particular god's will and because it isn't absolute or divinely inspired, it is immoral or amoral.

As for Humanists, we regard our way of thinking about morality as superior and we think their attempts to demonize our ethics speak more to the flaws in their own system than to any fundamental problem in ours.

I Think, Therefore I Am

Humanism is not just a philosophy; it's an overall approach to living a happy and fulfilling life. One part of this approach is our adherence to compassion-based ethical values. The other part is how we actually go about thinking through problems.

We Humanists aren't concerned so much with what people think about as much as we are with how people think. Or specifically, how well people think. And yes, thinking well is a discipline that requires effort.

As with Humanist morality, we consider this first and foremost a personal practice. Something we aspire to. We encourage others to practice critical thinking skills simply because of how much better your thinking and therefore your problem solving is when you employ these techniques. Just as with morality, if you choose to think in less rigorous ways, that's fine too. You are the one who has to live with the consequences.

Reality Matters

When it comes to thinking through our problems, Humanists are very much concerned with discerning, as much as possible, the real cause of our difficulties. We know that the closer our understanding of a problem is to the actual reality of what is causing it, the better our solutions will be.

Reality matters. Understanding the difference between what is real and what you imagine to be real determines whether you will be able to solve your problem, or whether you will instead spin your wheels and possibly make your problem worse.

For instance, if you have a field that needs water, and you think it isn't raining because your god is mad at you, your solution to that problem is going to be to try to appease your god. This is traditionally done through some sort of sacrifice or ritual prayer.

If, on the other hand, by using critical thinking, science and logic, you determine that it isn't raining because of weather patterns beyond your control, you are more likely to look for alternatives to your problem and perhaps figure out a way to irrigate your field instead.

While this example is obvious to pretty much everyone with even the slightest bit of education, the power of this reality-based approach manifests in areas where the boundaries between what is known and what is not known are less clear.

Critical Thinking

In order to better determine what is real vs. what is imagined, Humanists employ a variety of critical thinking skills. Our goal is to best determine what is real and true so we are constantly testing our own thinking. We are skeptical of claims until they are proven. We apply the rules of logic to make sure we aren't coming to any false conclusions. We prefer objective knowledge to subjective knowledge. And above all, we practice Freethought as a way to ensure that we challenge our own assumptions as rigorously as we challenge the assumptions of others.

Skepticism

This first aspect of thinking critically is to be skeptical. While most people think of skepticism as a negative practice, Humanists think of it as a very positive one. We know there is a truth out there and that we have the ability to figure out what that is. We aren't willing to allow ourselves to put our trust into something or someone just because what they are selling sounds good. We want to know if it actually works before we lay our money down.

When we are searching for a solution to a problem we research all our options. When we come across someone who says they have a solution, we apply a healthy dose of skepticism and research their claims. What do their critics think of their work? Do they have any testable and verifiable science to back up their claims? These are all reasonable questions to ask of someone who is claiming that they can solve our problems. If they can't answer them to our satisfaction, we look elsewhere. Again, this isn't a negative process unless you are invested in a solution that hasn't been proven to work because you are either the person selling it, or the person buying it.

Logic And Science

When evaluating claims, Humanists rely on the twin disciplines of logic and science. Logic helps us determine whether our own or someone else's arguments in support of a claim are valid. Science helps us determine whether the premises in the argument are even true in the first place.

We consider these skills to be useful in every aspect of our lives. From what shampoo we buy to the food we choose to eat to what politicians we choose to vote for. All around us people are making claims and it benefits us to know whether those claims are both logical and scientifically sound.

Freethought

Freethought is considered a central discipline for Humanist thought because your ability to think critically is limited without it. The term Freethought is often used interchangeably with "critical thinking" and that's because they both use the same skill set. But I like to treat Freethought as its own process because at the heart of Freethinking is the willingness to challenge your own assumptions. And that is perhaps the hardest aspect of thinking critically.

Freethinkers refuses to limit their thinking. We reject as arbitrary all social taboos, accepted wisdom and biases, and we challenge ourselves to think beyond those limitations to determine whether they are valid or not. Again, our goal is to discern what is true and what is real. If we limit ourselves to what is known and accepted, and if we aren't willing to challenge our own assumptions and biases, we will never be able to solve our most intractable problems.

Cockeyed Optimism

The last thing you should know about Humanism is that it is optimistic. In fact, we Humanists can seem a bit cockeyed at times. That's just an illusion though because we Humanists do actively and rigorously engage in critical thinking and so are often a bit more aware of what is possible than others might realize.

One of the main reasons we encourage optimism in ourselves and in others is because we know that optimism is the key to our motivation to act. Without a positive belief that we can make a difference we have no impetus to try. And unless we act, we will continue to be mired in the current status quo. I'm not sure about your life, but mine always seems to be in need of improvement.

So, let's look at the various aspects of how Humanists use and cultivate optimism.

I Can Do Anything You Can Do Better

Humanists are, generally speaking, unwilling to accept the status quo if the status quo involves suffering of any kind. We don't normally talk about sin, but if there is a sin in this life, it surely involves suffering unnecessarily. As Albert Camus once said,

"Perhaps we cannot prevent this world from being a world in which children are tortured. But we can reduce the number of tortured children. And if you don't help us, who else in the world can help us do this?"
— Albert Camus, *The Unbeliever and the Christians*

As far as we Humanists are concerned, suffering is not noble and we rarely learn anything useful from it. It's painful and we would like to avoid it as much as possible.

For the record, we don't just feel that way about our own suffering. We feel that way about others' as well. In fact, our own misery is in many ways easier to tolerate because it is happening to us. Watching others endure hardship is virtually intolerable.

Anyway, because we don't like to see harm come to others, and we don't like to experience unnecessary pain ourselves, we are always looking for ways in which we can improve what we are doing and make life better for everyone.

Whatever it is we are doing now, we are sure there is a better, more effective and efficient way to do it. And yes, we may be overly optimistic. But it is the refusal to accept the status quo and a belief that we can do better that drives innovation. All innovation.

If you don't believe you can do better, there is no reason to try. Believe you can and you pretty much have the responsibility to make an effort. This may be the reason why so many Nobel Laureates are professed Humanists. Even though there aren't very many of us in society, we are so active in pushing for innovation and progress that our influence greatly outweighs our numbers.

The Future's So Bright I've Got To Wear Shades

The second important aspect of our optimism is our focus on the future. Humanists are almost all Futurists. We enjoy thinking about what the future may be like. We enjoy thinking that there may come a time when equality is a reality; when disease and illness are things of the past; when we are able to live together in peace and harmony with goodwill towards all. And of course, we can envision a time when we are living in a sustainable way in harmony with nature.

Even though we can imagine such a future, that doesn't mean we think it would be easy to get there or that it is even possible to achieve. Though we may, at times, have our heads in the clouds, Humanism is an incredibly pragmatic philosophy. We understand the difference between having an ideal you are aiming for and what you might actually achieve. We just feel that it is better to have an ideal to work towards than to abandon the present to despair.

We are willing to work towards our goals incrementally, one step at a time. Baby steps if that's what it takes, as long as we keep pushing towards that ideal future. And yes, it takes time. And yes, it requires attitudes to change. But look at all we have accomplished so far:

- Slavery is now considered morally wrong pretty much everywhere.
- Skin color is no longer a socially acceptable way to judge people.
- Women are not only able to vote and own property, they can also work and enter into any field of endeavor they want (in Western countries).
- Education is now considered a universal right for all children everywhere.
- The death penalty has been abolished in most countries.
- Torture is now considered a crime against humanity.
- Despite all the setbacks and problems, the world community is working together on a wide variety of projects that would have been unimaginable just a couple of decades ago.
- The concept of Human Rights, just 50 years old, is now an accepted legal doctrine and something people everywhere demand for themselves.

And that's just a few of the advances in the social arena. When we look at the advances in medicine and science, the list of achievements is astonishing. And they are all fairly recent. From our perspective, the future is indeed bright.

Stand And Deliver

The most powerful aspect of the Humanist philosophy is that it encourages us to take responsibility for our lives and for the lives of those around us. We alone are responsible to make things better. If we don't, who will?

The great thing about responsibility is that once you embrace it, you are empowered to act. And by acting, you inspire others to take responsibility as well. The great lesson of Humanism is that you don't need everyone. Just a few committed people are enough to create societal change on a global scale.

Humanism is a progressive philosophy of life that, without supernaturalism, affirms our ability and responsibility to lead ethical lives of personal fulfillment that aspire to the greater good of humanity. It is a commitment to act according to our highest ideals and to work towards the betterment of humanity. It is a commitment to stand and deliver on the promise of the future.

While we realize we may not be able achieve our ideal future, Humanists are committed to getting as close to that ideal as possible. And if you won't help us, who will?

Resources

There are organizations and a wide variety of resources that can help you explore the philosophy of Humanism further. I also encourage you to check out my other books and online resources I have made available at www.jen-hancock.com

Online Resources

These resources can be found on the web.

- Humanist Manifesto III - published in 2003 by the American Humanist Association: http://www.americanhumanist.org/Who_We_Are/About_Humanism/Humanist_Manifesto_III
- Essays in Humanism - a journal published by the American Humanist Association: http://www.essaysinhumanism.org/
- The Genesis of a Humanist Manifesto - by Edwin H Wilson: http://www.infidels.org/library/modern/edwin_wilson/manifesto/index.html
- Books Published by the Humanist Press: http://evolvefish.com/fish/HumanistPress.html
- Humanist Books from Prometheus Books: http://www.prometheusbooks.com/index.php?main_page=index&cPath=35_31

- More online essays from the American Humanist Association: http://www.americanhumanist.org/Who_We_Are/About_Humanism
- The Humanist Tradition from the British Humanist Association: http://www.humanism.org.uk/humanism/humanist-tradition
- Introduction to Humanism video series by Jennifer Hancock: http://www.youtube.com/playlist?list=PL926B6F22CBF88997
- Humanist Heritage provides background on the history of Humanism in the UK: http://humanistheritage.org.uk/
- Humanistic Text has a great list of ancient Humanistic writings: www.humanistictexts.org

Books:

Here are some books on Humanism you might find interesting. You should be able to find these books wherever books are sold.

- The Way of Ethical Humanism - Gerald Larue

- Humanism as the Next Step - Mary & Lloyd Morain

- The Philosophy of Humanism - Corliss Lamont

- Freethinkers: A history of American Secularism - Susan Jacoby

- Good Without God - Greg Epstein

- Humanism and Democratic Criticism by Edward Said

- The Humanist Approach to Happiness: Practical Wisdom by Jennifer Hancock

- Humanism for Parents by Sean Curley

- Raising Freethinkers by Dale McGowan

Charities

Humanists are very philanthropic minded. It is part of our philosophy that we should try to help make the world a better place. Here are some Humanist charities that raise money to aid people in disasters and for other causes. All in the name of Humanism.

- Humanist Charities run by the American Humanist Association: http://www.humanistcharities.org/

- Foundation Beyond Belief: http://foundationbeyondbelief.org/

- Humanist Kiva Lending Group:
  http://www.kiva.org/team/humanist

Organizations:

If you are looking for a local Humanist group, please check out the national and international organizations to find a group in your area.

- The International Humanist and Ethical Union: http://www.iheu.org/ Has a list of organizations by country.

- The British Humanist Association: http://www.humanism.org.uk/home

- The American Humanist Association: http://www.americanhumanist.org/

The are also several Humanistic groups available. For instance:

- The American Ethical Union: http://www.aeu.org/

- The Society for Humanistic Judaism: http://www.shj.org/

- The Center for Inquiry, which hosts the Council for Secular Humanism: http://www.centerforinquiry.net/

- The HUUmanists, Humanists within the UUA: http://www.huumanists.org/

About the Author:

Jennifer Hancock is a writer, speaker and Humanist.

Her other books include: The Humanist Approach to Happiness: Practical Wisdom.

Jennifer also has a variety of online resource and training materials available at her website .

She can be found on the web at
http://www.jen-hancock.com/

~~~~~

Connect with Me Online:

Twitter: http://twitter.com/#!/JentheHumanist

Facebook: http://www.facebook.com/JentheHumanist

Or sign up for my mailing list:
http://eepurl.com/c3LuI

Made in the USA
Las Vegas, NV
18 February 2022

44149959R00046